STEPHEN SONDHEIM BROADWAY SOLOS

T0085037

CONTENTS

THE CD IS PLAYABLE ON ANY CD PLAYER, AND IS ALSO ENHANCED SO MAC AND PC USERS CAN ADJUST THE RECORDING TO ANY TEMPO WITHOUT CHANGING THE PITCH.

ISBN 978-1-4234-7278-0

RILTING MUSIC, INC.

EXCLUSIVELY DISTRIBUTED BY

HAL•LEONARD®
CORPORATION

7777 W. BLUEMOUND RD. P.O. BOX 13819 MILWAUKEE, WI 53213

Visit Hal Leonard Online at
www.halleonard.com

ANYONE CAN WHISTLE

from ANYONE CAN WHISTLE

1/2

CLARINET

Words and Music by
STEPHEN SONDHEIM

BEING ALIVE
from COMPANY

Music and Lyrics by
STEPHEN SONDHEIM

CLARINET

3/4

BROADWAY BABY

from FOLLIES

5/6

CLARINET

Music and Lyrics by
STEPHEN SONDHEIM

CHILDREN WILL LISTEN
from INTO THE WOODS

CLARINET

Words and Music by
STEPHEN SONDHEIM

COMEDY TONIGHT

from A FUNNY THING HAPPENED ON THE WAY TO THE FORUM

Words and Music by
STEPHEN SONDHEIM

9/10

CLARINET

GOOD THING GOING
from MERRILY WE ROLL ALONG

CLARINET

Words and Music by
STEPHEN SONDHEIM

JOHANNA
from SWEENEY TODD

Words and Music by
STEPHEN SONDHEIM

CLARINET

LOSING MY MIND

from FOLLIES

CLARINET

Music and Lyrics by
STEPHEN SONDHEIM

NOT A DAY GOES BY
from MERRILY WE ROLL ALONG

Words and Music by
STEPHEN SONDHEIM

CLARINET

NOT WHILE I'M AROUND
from SWEENEY TODD

CLARINET

Words and Music by
STEPHEN SONDHEIM

OLD FRIENDS
from MERRILY WE ROLL ALONG

CLARINET

Words and Music by
STEPHEN SONDHEIM

PRETTY WOMEN

from SWEENEY TODD

CLARINET

Words and Music by
STEPHEN SONDHEIM

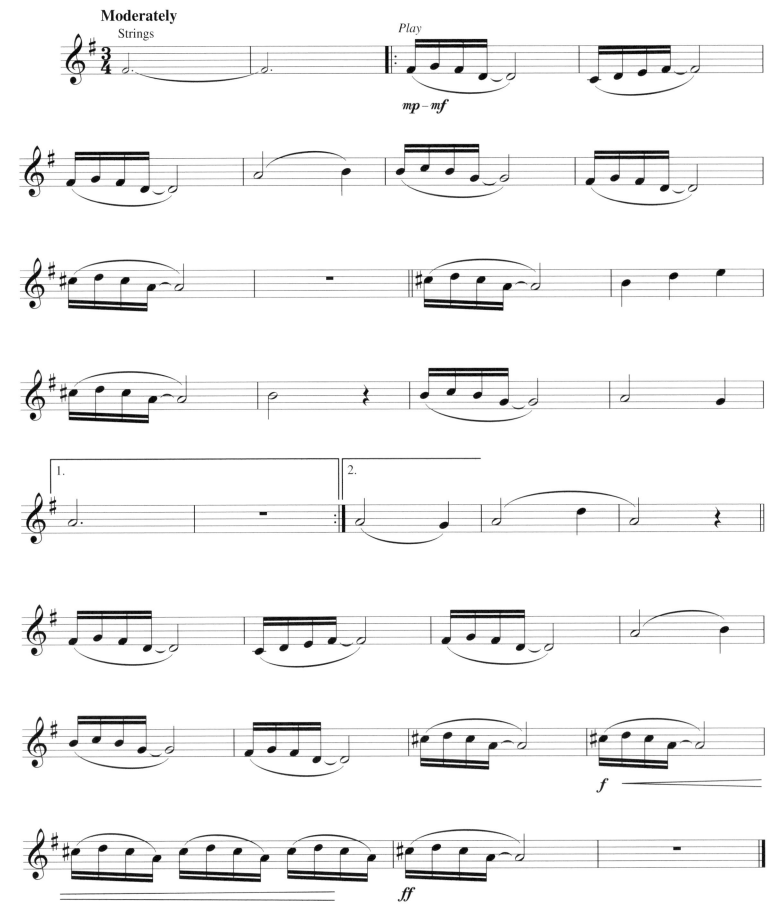

SEND IN THE CLOWNS

from the Musical A LITTLE NIGHT MUSIC

Words and Music by
STEPHEN SONDHEIM

CLARINET

Slowly, with feeling

SUNDAY
from SUNDAY IN THE PARK WITH GEORGE

CLARINET

Words and Music by
STEPHEN SONDHEIM